1949

Superaccurate atomic clock invented by Isidor Rabi in the United States.

1884

Greenwich Meridian (imaginary line) chosen as WITHDRAW starting point for measuring time all around the world.

1927

Quartz clock invented by Americans W. A Marrison and J.W. Horton.

2014

Team of U.S. scientists builds Strontium Lattice atomic clock. It is predicted to keep perfect time for 5 billion years.

1728-1761

British carpenter John Harrison invents chronometers to keep accurate time on long voyages.

Calendars Around the World

Our Calendar's Based on the...

...Sun!

...Moon!

...Sun and moon!

Ancient Egyptians, Athenians

Arabs, Muslims

Ancient Chinese, Jews

...Sun, moon, and planet Venus!

Clocks and watches show us time passing, whereas calendars are ways of organizing time. They measure, record, and predict time past, present, and future. Calendars can be written down, carved in stone, programmed on computers, or stored in people's memories.

At different times and in different places, people invented all kinds of calendars. Some were based on observations of the Sun, moon, planets, and stars. Some followed the seasons of the year. Some counted time from important events. Many were based on religious beliefs, myths, and legends.

Aztec calendar stone,
Central America, ca. 1500 CE

Author:

Fiona Macdonald studied history at Cambridge University and at the University of East Anglia, both in England. She has taught adult education, and in schools and universities, and is the author of numerous books for children on historical topics.

Artist:

David Antram was born in Brighton, England, in 1958. He studied at Eastbourne College of Art and then worked in advertising for 15 years before becoming a full-time artist. He has illustrated many children's nonfiction books.

Series creator:

David Salariya was born in Dundee, Scotland. He has illustrated a wide range of books and has created and designed many new series for publishers in the UK and overseas. David established The Salariya Book Company in 1989. He lives in Brighton, England, with his wife, illustrator Shirley Willis, and their son, Jonathan.

Editor: Caroline Coleman

Editorial Assistant: Mark Williams

PAPER FROM

SUSTAINABLE
FORESTS

© The Salariya Book Company Ltd MMXVI

Published in Great Britain in 2016 by
The Salariya Book Company Ltd
25 Marlborough Place, Brighton BN1 1UB

ISBN-13: 978-0-531-21928-7 (lib. bdg.) 978-0-531-22052-8 (pbk.)

Published in 2016 in the United States
by Franklin Watts
An imprint of Scholastic Inc.
Published simultaneously in Canada.

A CIP catalog record for this book is available from the Library of Congress.

Printed and bound in China.
Printed on paper from sustainable sources.

1 2 3 4 5 6 7 8 9 10 R 25 24 23 22 21 20 19 18 17 16

You Wouldn't Want to Live Without™
Clocks and Calendars!

Written by
Fiona Macdonald

Illustrated by
David Antram

Series created by
David Salariya

Franklin Watts®
An Imprint of Scholastic Inc.

Contents

Introduction   5

Years and Seasons   6

Months, Weeks, Days, Hours…   8

The First Time Machines   10

Go With the Flow   12

Blowing in the Wind   14

Around and Around   16

Side to Side   18

You Can Take It With You   20

Time Around the World   22

Clockwatching   24

Just a Minute…   26

Time Rules   28

Glossary   30

Index   32

Introduction

Imagine, if you can, a world without clocks and calendars, where no one knew what time it was, which day of the week, or even which year! Buses, trains, and planes would run late, stores would not know when to open, and school classes could not begin or end on time. There would be no holidays, no festivals—and no birthdays. You would not even know how old you were! Luckily, for the past 30,000 years—maybe longer—ingenious men and women have figured out ways to measure and keep track of time, using many different clocks and calendars. We owe them all a big "thank you!" Read on, and find out more…

Most people nowadays might not know what this ancient timekeeping device is, or how to use it. But these old-fashioned sundials paved the way for clocks as we know them today.

Years and Seasons

You're a Stone Age hunter. You survive by killing buffalo that run past your camp every summer. You store the meat carefully, to make it last all winter. But by springtime, you're hungry, and need to know when the buffalo will return. You look for clues that summer's coming: green grass growing, longer daylight hours, changing stars in the sky. Once these appear, the buffalo should come back again. You remember this information, and make drawings and carvings to record it. Congratulations! You've invented the world's first calendar!

Waaah! I want my dinner!

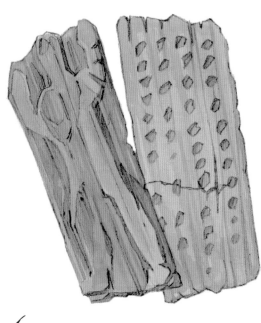

SIGN OF THE TIMES. The oldest surviving calendar (left), carved on mammoth tusk more than 30,000 years ago, shows the constellation Orion (on the left side) and a nine-month pregnancy timetable (on the right side).

STAR SPOTTERS. The ancient Borana calendar from East Africa was based on observing the moon and seven special stars or star groups (right). It is accurate, and is still used today.

Too late! Missed them!

Top Tip

Look for clues to the changing seasons of the year: migrating birds, blossoming flowers, high tides, and river floods!

PREHISTORIC PUZZLE.
The Stone Circle at Callanish, Isle of Lewis, Scotland, was built ca. 3000 BCE, as a calendar, or a temple, or a tomb.

CACTUS CALENDAR.
Before paper was invented, Native American peoples recorded important events on calendar sticks made of dried cactus.

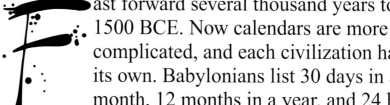

Months, Weeks, Days, Hours...

Whose Day Is It Anyway?

ANCIENT EGYPTIANS said that each new day started at dawn.

Fast forward several thousand years to 1500 BCE. Now calendars are more complicated, and each civilization has its own. Babylonians list 30 days in a month, 12 months in a year, and 24 hours in a day. Jewish calendars have weeks of seven days. Egyptian years last for 360 days plus five "extras." Today, we still use these ancient calendars to plan our busy lives, but many other old ways of organizing time have almost been forgotten. How would you like to follow these calendar traditions: weeks with 4 days (Africa), days with 10 hours (China), and years with 18 months (Central America)?

BABYLONIANS and ancient Greeks, Jews, and Muslims believed that days started at nightfall.

Cockadoodledoo

ANCIENT ROMAN and Chinese days started at midnight.

MAYA AND AZTEC days began at noon, when the Sun was highest in the sky.

FARMERS' days began when roosters started crowing. The noise made it hard to sleep.

9

The First Time Machines

See! It's very simple, just a stick and a half-circle dial carved on stone. But it tells the time for all to see, as long as the Sun is shining. It's a sundial—the world's first machine for measuring time. Sundials were invented in ancient Egypt around 5,500 years ago and are still used today. They work by casting a shadow. From dawn to dusk, as the Sun seems to move across the sky, the shadow moves as well, pointing to the hours marked on the dial.

HANDY! Keep track of time like an ancient Egyptian: divide daylight into 12 hours. That way, you can count the hours on one hand. It's easy—try it!

3 segments

$3 \times 4 = 12$

4 fingers

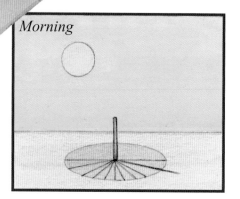

How to Read a Sundial

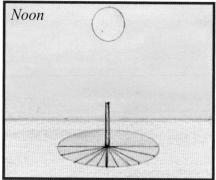

Morning

Noon

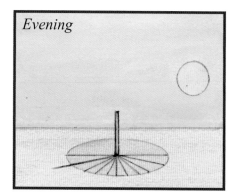

Evening

THE SUN appears low in the sky. Its slanting light casts a long shadow that moves around from the start of the dial.

THE SUN appears high overhead. Its light casts a short, strong shadow right on the midpoint of the dial.

THE SUN appears to sink down. The sundial shadow grows longer and moves toward the endpoint of the dial.

Go With the Flow

Wonderful Water?

WATER CLOCKS usually work well—but not always. They need a steady flow of water.

Time never stands still! That's why the first clockmakers, in Greece, Egypt, Asia, and America, use substances that move at a regular rate to measure time. Most choose flowing water; others prefer sand or mercury (a liquid metal). They all know that a fixed amount of their chosen substance will always take the same time to run from one place to another. Let's visit Greece around 350 BCE to see a clepsydra (water clock) in action. Water clocks are used to time speeches at Greek assemblies—an essential part of democracy!

WATER PRESSURE is also important.

THEY also need to be repaired regularly.

FREEZING winters can cause problems.

A WATER CLOCK can tell you only the amount of time that has gone by—it can't tell you what time of day it is, like a sundial can.

Now they tell me! It's a clock!

IN ANCIENT PERSIA (Iran) clocks are bowls with holes. If you drop one into water, it always takes the same time to sink.

You Can Do It!

Make holes in a plastic pot. (Ask an adult for help.) Put it in a bowl of water, then time how long it takes to fill and sink. Now you can use it as a water clock!

Stopped by the clock! What a wonderful invention!

Blowing in the Wind

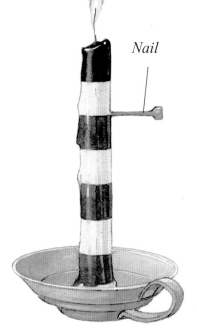

Nail

Don't want a water clock? Then how about a candle? They burn at a slow, steady rate, ideal for measuring time. They're simple to use and easy to carry from place to place. Unlike sundials, they work indoors and in the dark as well. Since around 500 CE, they've been replacing old-style oil lamps, which people have used for centuries. But candles aren't cheap. They drip. They don't burn for long. They can cause fires. They can't tell the exact time—not even whether it's morning or afternoon. And if the flame blows out, they're useless!

ROYAL REMINDER.
England's King Alfred (849–899 CE) turned candles into alarm clocks by adding nails. As the wax melted, the nails fell out, clinked noisily on the candleholder, and woke him.

SWEET AND SLOW.
In Asia, precious incense burned slowly and gently and was used to measure time. It smelled good, too!

TIME FLIES!
Hourglasses filled with trickling sand were safer than burning lamps or candles. They were good timekeepers, except on ships in a storm!

How It Works

Around 900 CE, Arab mathematician Al-Battani proved that a year has 365 days, 5 hours, 46 minutes, 24 seconds. That varies only slightly from what we know to be true today.

LOST YOUR LIGHT? Then listen for the night watchman. He tells people when to go to bed and when to get up again.

SAY YOUR PRAYERS—it's a good way of counting time. Old books told cooks which prayer was best for each recipe.

Around and Around

It's the year 1300 in Europe, and there's been a timekeeping revolution. We've got mechanical clocks! Look, high on that tower, a clock face made of metal! Now, see that heavy weight? Slowly, steadily, it's being pulled down by gravity. It's linked by a rope to wheels and gears. As the weight sinks down, the gears move a metal rod. That turns another wheel and it moves the clock hand around the dial. When the weight reaches the ground, strong men wind it back to the top of the tower. Excellent engineering!

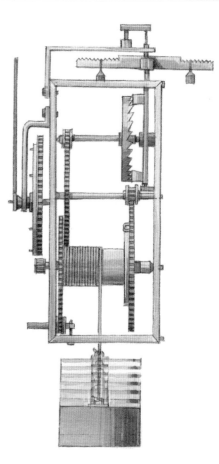

TEETH AND TIME.
The toothed wheel turns; the rod moves the balance wheel; the balance wheel moves the clock hand.

Balance wheel

Rod

Toothed wheel

WEIGHT AND POWER.
Mechanical clocks are powered by weights of metal or stone. Weights need to be carefully balanced, or the clock will run fast or slow.

GEAR UP! Mechanical clocks measure time by a steady flow of little movements. These are controlled and transmitted by notched wheels, called gears.

Prague astronomical clock, ca. 1410

How It Works

Our word *clock* comes from an old French word, *cloche*, meaning "bell." This came about because before mechanical clocks, monks rang church bells to announce prayer time.

TICKTOCK.
Mechanical clocks have brought a new sound to the world: a steady "ticktock" that tells everyone time is passing.

Clang!

These new clocks are very noisy neighbors!

Side to Side

S woosh! Swoosh! The sound of genius! We're in Italy, it's 1641, and brilliant mathematician Galileo Galilei has just designed a clock with a pendulum. That's a weight swinging from side to side: another regular, steady movement useful for measuring time. Galileo's clock will never be built, but his studies will inspire a great Dutch scientist, Christiaan Huygens, to create the first pendulum clock in 1657. Pendulum clocks are so accurate—and look so grand—that all rich Europeans want one! They're the best timekeepers invented so far.

LIGHT FANTASTIC. Galileo observed a heavy church lamp swinging from side to side. Each swing was the same length, and took an equal amount of time.

THIS GAVE Galileo the idea for a pendulum clock. Below is a modern model of a clock based on his 1641 design.

Pendulum

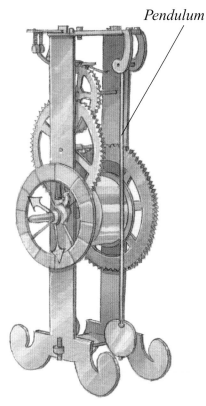

THE CHRISTIAN CALENDAR is no longer accurate, so Pope Gregory XIII introduces a new calendar in 1582. When Britain adopts the calendar in 1752, there are riots, because Gregory's calendar "loses" 11 days—people want them back!

MINUTES (60 per hour) and seconds (60 per minute) begin to be widely used in timekeeping. Soon, clocks are fitted with minute hands. Second hands are added later, around 1780.

How It Works

Galileo discovered that the time it takes a pendulum to swing depends on how long it is. This makes a pendulum very useful for measuring time.

No excuses for being late, now that we've got a pendulum clock!

19

You Can Take It With You

Let's stay in early modern Europe for a while, because it's home to yet another clever timekeeping invention. Around 1450, expert metalworkers in Germany begin to make locks that open with keys that unwind a spring. After several accidents—springs can be dangerous!— they realize that the energy stored in a coiled spring can also be used for timekeeping. If the spring unwinds gently and steadily, it can measure time and turn the hands of a clock. Springs are small, so spring-powered clocks can be light and portable. Now, around 1550, they're the world's first watches!

Spring

SIMPLE BUT POWERFUL. A coil spring is a length of metal or wire wound into a spiral (left). Springs store energy, and then release it as they unwind.

WATCH THIS! Springs wound with a key were used to turn wheels, gears, and balance wheels (see page 16), and move the hands of clocks.

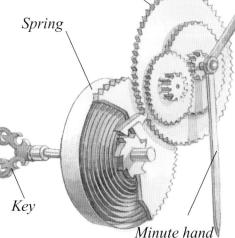

Gears
Hour hand
Spring
Key
Minute hand

You Can Do It!

Coil a pipe cleaner into a spring, then hold it between your fingertips. Can you feel the stored energy in the spring pushing against them?

Think of it as a surprise gift, Your Majesty!

DON'T BE LATE. Without a watch, you'll find it difficult to check the time when you are out and about, in town or out in the country.

TIME FOR ACTION. Soldiers, synchronize your watches! After about 1900, cheap watches worn by troops made battle planning easier.

STATUS SYMBOL. A fine pocket watch with a fancy gold chain showed that the wearer was well organized, fashionable, and wealthy.

Time Around the World

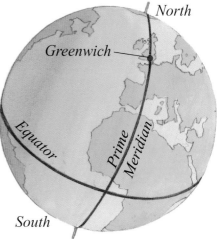

You're a traveler or explorer, far out at sea or in the middle of a desert. And you're lost! You can estimate your position north or south from the angle of the Sun. But east or west? That's hopeless! What you need is an ultrareliable clock—a chronometer. Set the chronometer to the right time when you start your journey. Then, as you travel, see what time the chronometer shows at noon when the Sun is highest in the sky. The difference between chronometer time and local time, measured by the Sun, will let you calculate how far east or west you've traveled.

TIME LINE. In 1884, governments agreed to measure world time starting from a Meridian (imaginary line) passing through Greenwich, England.

LOCAL TIME, measured by the Sun, changes by one hour for every 15 degrees traveled east or west. But time that is measured by clocks stays the same.

ENGLISH CARPENTER John Harrison spent more than 30 years (1728–1761) perfecting his spring-powered chronometers. They kept excellent time, even on long sea voyages.

EARLY RAILROADS had a problem: different local times! "Railroad time," using just one clock for a whole rail network, began in Britain in 1840.

You Can Do It!

Be a virtual time traveler! Using the Internet or a library, can you find out what time it is in New York when it is noon in London?

That can't be the 8:38!

TRAVEL TIME DISASTER! In 1853, two American passenger trains collided because the guards had set their watches to different local times in their hometowns.

Clockwatching

Are you a good timekeeper? If so, would you like to live around 1900, in a busy, dirty city in Europe or the United States? You'll see clocks everywhere: in stations, stores, offices, and factories. That's because workers must arrive on time, and not waste a second dawdling! Tight time schedules also make sure that factory machines run smoothly. Away from work, clocks will soon become part of twentieth-century life for everyone. War and peace, medicine, technology, sports, and entertainment will be unthinkable without them.

Top Tip

Get organized! Learn to manage your time! You can start by making a list. It might contain urgent tasks to finish, new books to read, or your future ambitions.

MEDIA TIME. Have you heard them? Time signals occur at the start of television and radio broadcasts.

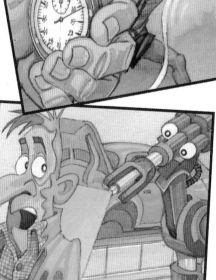

SPORTS TIME. Old-style stopwatches and modern digital clocks time record-breaking races.

LIFE TIME. Medical monitors use timers to check your pulse, heartbeat, and other signs of life.

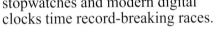

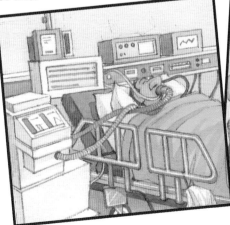

SPACE TIME. Rocket launches and space flights rely on clocks for split-second timing.

WORKING TO TIME. Timers can control tasks performed by automatic robots.

Just a Minute...

Pendulum clocks are good, chronometers are better—but twentieth-century inventions have changed timekeeping forever. Quartz clocks (1927) and atomic clocks (1949) still use steady, repeated movements to measure time. But now these movements are super-fast: atoms in an atomic clock "flip" 9,192,631,770 times per second! Atomic clocks are extraordinarily accurate, and quartz clocks are amazing in a different way. They're so cheap to mass-produce that most electronic devices are fitted with one. How many can you spot in your home or school?

DO YOU WEAR a quartz watch? If so, it works this way. Electric current from a battery (1) makes a quartz crystal (2) vibrate 32,768 times per second.

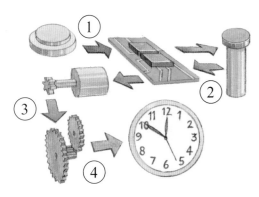

THE VIBRATION powers a tiny electric motor (3). This turns gears and wheels (4), and they measure time and move the watch hands.

STAY RIGHT ON TIME. Signals from atomic clocks control time-keeping devices in computers, phones, and GPS systems all around the world.

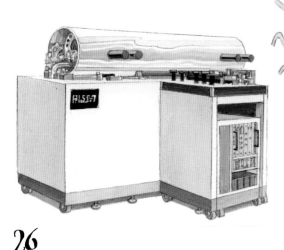

Check your watch or clock against atomic time! You can see live signals from a U.S. Navy atomic clock on the U.S. Naval Observatory Web site: http://tycho. usno.navy.mil/ simpletime.html

$$E = MC^2$$

STRANGE BUT TRUE. Atomic clocks helped investigate time itself. In experiments on jet planes in 1971, they tested a theory (above) from scientist Albert Einstein.

EINSTEIN was right! Atomic clocks proved that time does not pass steadily, but speeds up or slows down, depending on how fast we are moving.

Time Rules

T oday, almost everything we do is timed to the last minute. And we like to do those things quickly! For working, studying, eating, playing, downloading data, or just messaging friends, fast is fantastic! In many ways, that's great. There's so much to achieve and enjoy if we can organize our time. But, just sometimes, it can seem as if clever timekeeping devices are ruling our lives.

If you could choose, which would you prefer: fast-paced modern life, or a world without clocks and calendars?

Relaxation time

Dinnertime

Homework time

Sports time

Tick tock

Music time

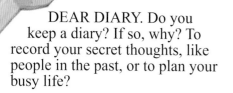

DEAR DIARY. Do you keep a diary? If so, why? To record your secret thoughts, like people in the past, or to plan your busy life?

IN CONTROL? There's nothing like a timetable to organize work, travel, and holidays. But too much information can sometimes be overwhelming…

You Can Do It!

Alligator clips with leads

Big potato

Copper wire

Galvanized nails

1.5V battery-powered clock, battery removed

Follow this diagram (above) to make your own potato-powered clock.

Brrriiinnng!

Breakfast time

Schooltime

Bus time

Lunchtime

NONSTOP CLOCK.
The 24-hour clock was designed around 1400 CE, in Italy. Now it's used worldwide, for travel, in hospitals, and by armed forces, to avoid dangerous confusion.

MOST ANALOG
(traditional) clocks still show 12 hours; the hands go around twice per day. Some modern digital clocks show 24 hours, in clear, simple numbering.

Glossary

Analog clock A timekeeping machine with a round face (dial) and either 12 or 24 numerals.

Atomic clock A clock that uses very rapidly changing states of energy in atoms to measure time.

Atoms Tiny particles, the smallest "building blocks" of matter. Everything in the world is made of them. There are 90 different natural atoms; scientists have created around 28 more.

Babylonian Belonging to a civilization based in ancient Babylon that reached the peak of its power around 1780 BCE.

Chronometer A very accurate clock or watch, originally designed for timekeeping and navigation at sea.

Clepsydra The ancient Greek name for a water clock. It means "water thief."

Clock time Time measured at a regular, unchanging rate by a watch or clock.

Constellation A pattern of stars in the night sky. Ancient peoples gave the patterns names.

Dial A flat circle or half circle, with divisions of time marked on it.

Flip (in atomic clocks) When parts of atoms change from one energy state to another.

Galvanized Coated with a thin layer of zinc (a shiny gray metal) for protection.

Gears Wheels with notches or "teeth" around the rim. They transmit force or movement from one part of a machine to another.

Gravity A natural force that pulls objects toward one another. Earth's gravity pulls all less massive (smaller, lighter) objects toward it.

Incense Resin (gum from trees) and other natural substances that produce sweet-smelling smoke when they are burned. Often used in religious ceremonies.

Local time Time measured by observation of the Sun. Unlike **clock time**, local time changes as we travel east or west around the world.

Meridian Imaginary line drawn around the Earth, passing through the North and South Poles.

Metronome Simple pendulum clock, used by musicians to keep time. The center of mass of the pendulum can be adjusted so that it beats faster or slower.

Observation Careful looking, measuring, and recording.

Olympiad A period of four years, starting from 776 BCE (the legendary date of the first Olympic Games). It was used to count years in ancient Greece.

Pendulum A weight hanging from a fixed point so it can swing freely from back to front or side to side.

Quartz Silicon dioxide; a very common white mineral found as crystals in the earth.

Railroad time Standardized time used by a whole railroad network, for safety and to avoid confusion.

Transmit Carry, pass along.

Tusk An overgrown tooth. Mammoth tusks could grow 16 feet (5 meters) long.

Vibration Shaking. Regular vibrations are sometimes used to measure time, for example, in quartz watches.

Index

A
Africa 6, 8
Al-Battani 15
Alfred, King 14
Asia 12

B
balance wheel 16, 20–21
bells 17
books 15

C
calendars
  ancient 8–9
  traditions 8–9
Callanish, Stone Circle 7
China 8–9
chronometer 22, 26
clocks
  alarm 14
  analog 29
  astronomical 17
  atomic 26–27
  candle 14–15
  digital 25, 29
  hands 18–19, 20–21
  mechanical 16–17
  pendulum 18–19, 26
  quartz 26
  spring-powered 20–21
  24-hour 29
  water 12–13, 14
constellations 6

E
Egypt 10–11, 12
Einstein, Albert 27
England 22–23

G
Galilei, Galileo 18, 19
gears 16, 20
Germany 20
Greece 9, 12
Greenwich 22–23
Gregory XIII, Pope 18

H
Harrison, John 22
Huygens, Christiaan 18

I
Italy 18, 29

K
keys 20–21

L
lamps
  church 18
  oil 14
locks 20
London 23

M
Meridian line 22
moon 6

N
New York 23

P
pendulum 18, 19
Prague astronomical clock 17
prayer 15, 17

R
railroads 23

S
scientists 18, 27
Scotland 7
seasons 6–7
stars 6
summer 6–7
sundials 10–11, 14

T
time
  atomic 27
  clock 22
  local 22–23
  railroad 23

W
watches 20–21, 23, 25
winter 6–7, 12

Keeping Time

Two of the world's most popular activities, sports and music, depend on accurate timekeeping.

Winner by a hair. The time difference between top athletes in a race can be less than $\frac{1}{100}$ of a second. That's much, much less time than it takes to say "clock" or "calendar."

- Joint decision. Quartz clocks used at Olympic competitions can measure $\frac{1}{1,000}$ of a second. But at the 1984 Los Angeles Olympics, two female swimmers were both declared winners. No one could measure any difference in their times.

- Gooooaaaal! Extra time for injuries or stoppages can make all the difference in a soccer match. In the 2013 UEFA Super Cup Final, both teams scored last-minute goals in the final extra moments. The winner (Bayern Munich) was eventually decided by a penalty shoot-out.

- All together. Members of bands and orchestras learn to play in time with one another. They practice with a metronome and read the composer's time indication on sheet music. At a concert, they are guided by a conductor and watch or listen for signals from one another.

- Feel the beat! To put extra emotion into their music, singers and instrumentalists often squeeze or stretch time. This can ruin a live performance—or make it extra exciting.

Top Clocks

- The world's most accurate clock is the Strontium Lattice Clock, made at the U.S. Joint Institute for Laboratory Astrophysics in 2014. The atoms inside flick 430 trillion times per second. It is predicted to keep perfect time for 5 billion years.

- The world's most expensive man's watch was sold in 2014 for $24.4 million. Crafted from real gold, the Graves Supercomplication model was designed for a U.S. businessman. The most expensive woman's watch is the Chopard 201, which features 874 diamonds of various colors, and costs $25 million.

- The Omega Speedmaster Professional is the only watch to have been worn on the moon. It was worn there by U.S. astronaut Buzz Aldrin in 1969.

- In 2012, the Rolex Deepsea Challenge watch set a new record for underwater timekeeping when it was carried 35,787 feet (10,908 m) below the sea surface, and worked well!

- The oldest clock still working is probably the astronomical clock at Salisbury Cathedral, England (though clocks in France and Italy also claim this record). It was made around 1386 and still keeps good time.